Life Insurance Sales Ammo

Table of Contents

Introduction

This manual is a collection of hundreds of sales tips and ideas from over 20 years of meetings, discussions and on the job practice.

It is extremely difficult to determine authorship of any of the sales ideas which are borrowed, adapted, modified and transformed over the years. You will likely find that while you might be able to associate one or several particular ideas to someone you may have heard or read, in most instances the origins of these ideas remain questionable.

Please accept this handbook as a portion of the collective wisdom of successful life insurance agents across the globe. If you find just one idea that sparks your next sale, then this handbook will have allowed you to help your clients protect their loved ones.

Questions
To Make The Sale

Building Interest

How much life Insurance have you purchased to protect your family?

If you knew your family would be protected if something were to happen to you, how would you feel?

How important is it to you that you have enough money to live on at retirement?

Which is more important to you right now, having enough money for retirement or protecting your family in case something were to happen to you?

What is your attitude about life insurance?

Would you have any objection to discussing your life insurance program with me?

How much life insurance have you bought for your family?

Which do you like least, taxes or life insurance?

How much life insurance do you think you will need when you die?

How long do you think you'll need your life insurance?

Have you thought about what effect taxes will have on your investments over the years?

If there were a way to force yourself to create great wealth, you'd probably want to know more about it wouldn't you?

How do you think your wife and family would feel knowing that they were protected if something were to happen to you?

How much is your life worth? How much did you insure it for? Would you trade?

Can I talk to you about the $500,000 I owe you?

How would you like to retire with a guaranteed income for the rest of your life?

How important would a comfortable retirement be to you?

We have the kind of life insurance that protects your family when you die, but we also have the kind that can help you save for a down payment on a house, college for your children, or retirement. Which kind would you prefer?

If there were a way to protect your family forever from the financial horrors of widowhood for just a few dollars a month you'd probably want to know more about it wouldn't you?

Would you object if I showed you something that might benefit you?

May I show you something that I think will work for you?

You don't mind if I ask you a few questions do you?

Do you feel success is accidental or planned?

Would you agree that where you are right now is based on past decisions? Would you be willing to make what seems like a difficult decision now that could improve you future?

If there were a way to reduce your widow's exposure to the financial horrors of inadequate life insurance with some low cost life insurance to begin with, you'd probably want to know more about it, wouldn't you?

What is your opinion about life insurance?

Are you interested in saving money?

If there were a way to force yourself to create great wealth for your family, you'd probably want to know more about it wouldn't you?

Building Rapport

What do you do for a living?

Where did you go to school?

Do you have any children?

How long have you been at your job?

Where are you from originally?

I see from the awards on your wall that you are a high achiever. What in your life made you such a high achiever? Do you agree that all great achievers are great planners? Do you feel success is accidental or planned?

How did you get into that particular business?

What part of the country do you come from originally?

What are some of your hobbies?

How long have you been a (golfer, tennis player, hunter, etc.)?

Would you tell me about your family?

Other than working where you do now, what other career experiences have you pursued?

Do you like living in (state name)?

Do you get to spend enough time with your family?

Are you enjoying your free-time activities?

Tell me about your children.

What type of recreational activities or hobbies do you and your family enjoy?

Goal Questions

What do you hope will happen when you retire?

What kind of results are you looking for from your investments?

What income would you need if you were retiring today, assuming your children have moved out of the house and your debts are paid?

Considering your needs now and in the future, what amount of insurance do you feel would be best for your family?

Are you more concerned with the return on your money or the return of you money?

How important would a comfortable retirement be to you?

How much money will you need to earn on a monthly basis to become financially independent?

What level of savings would be necessary?

What type of investments would you like to have?

What type of preparatory schools would you like for your child to attend?

How would you finance these schools?

What university would you direct your child towards?

What does this university cost to attend per year?

Have you saved any money yet?

How many children would you send to college?

What level of income increase would be necessary for you to send all your children to college?

What are your goals for retirement?

Are you committed to your goals?

Have you asked yourself why you haven't reached more of them?

When do you feel is the right time to start working toward your goals?

Are you worthy of more?

How strong is your desire?

What's the most exiting aspect of your job?

How do you see your responsibilities changing in the next 5 years?

What are your goals regarding your areas of responsibilities?

What do you think are the greatest challenges facing you and your organization over the next 6 months?

What do you plan to accomplish in the next 6 months?

What goals do you have in place for next year?

Why would achieving that goal be important to you?

What would achieving that goal mean to you?

What are your personal goals?

How did you determine that these were top priority goals?

What were your goals last year?

Which goal is more important to you next year?

How are you currently tracking the progress of your goals?

What is your time frame to achieve your goal?

What is preventing you from being where you want to be/?

What are the obstacles you are facing?

What challenges must be met before you can achieve what you have worked so hard for?

What are you doing to overcome _____?

Why haven't you achieved your goals?

Which obstacle is the most crucial for you to overcome?

Are you making the progress necessary to overcome the obstacles you face?

Do you feel there are other steps you might take in overcoming your obstacles?

Are you interested in overcoming the obstacles that seem to be holding you back?

Fact Finding Questions

Tell me about your benefits at work?

What's your greatest fear about retirement?

What's the best investment you've ever made?

What's the most important investment you've ever made?

Does your family have any history of health problems?

What do you like most about your benefits at work?

How much life insurance do you have at work?

What portion of your income comes from your assets and what portion from your salary?

How much money do you save per month? Are you happy with this amount?

About how much have you accumulated so far?

Do you leave your savings alone, or do you use them every once in a while for vacations, a new car or emergencies?

How much more would you like to save to help you accomplish your goals?

Are you like most people? Do you spend first, and then try to save? If so, there's probably not much left over.

Do you think your family will be able to live on what you've accumulated so far if something were to happen to you?
Outside of work, how much life insurance do you own?

Disturbing Questions

How important is it to you that your family has enough money to live on if something were to happen to you?

If your widow calls me tomorrow, what would you like me to tell her?

What would your life be like if you were unable to work?

Who do you want to raise your children in the event of your death? Will they be able to do it without additional money?

Are you planning to provide for your wife for as long as you live or as long as she lives?

If you had died today, and you could come back for five minutes to speak to your widow, could you do so without having to say "I'm sorry", or "I wish I had left you more money"?

What would your family's life be like if you weren't around?

Would your children still be able to go to college if you weren't around to help them pay for it?

What's the worst thing that you think might happen to your family if you were to die?

If you died tonight, and I stopped by in a few days, which of the following items would concern your spouse the most?
* Funeral costs?
* Unforeseen Expenses?
* Mortgage or rent?
* College Costs?
* Family Income?

How important would taking care of your family be if you weren't around?

Could you, right now give me 30% of everything you own in cash? That's the least Uncle Sam will take.

Are you going to be prepared to live the last 25 years of your life without a paycheck?

Who would be affected if you or your spouse were to die suddenly? What would happen financially to your family?

Are you interested in saving money?

If you were ever going to start saving money, when do you think would be the best time to start?

How do you intend to prevent your wife's second husband from becoming the heir to your estate instead of your children?

How much life insurance do you have at work?

Outside of work, how much life insurance do you own?

When are you going to start preparing for the old person you are going to be one day?

Why let the government take half of your estate when you die?

If there were a way to keep you out of the 90% who retire close to poverty, you'd probably want to know more about it wouldn't you?

How much life insurance would you buy for your family if you knew you were going to die tomorrow? How do you know you aren't going to?

Have you calculated what it would cost your family to be without enough life insurance?

Do you ever wonder why some people retire in comfort while other people live paycheck to paycheck? Are they just unlucky or do you think it was because of poor planning?

What do you like best about losing money? Just give me the top three things. Are you willing to take actions so that you can stop losing money?

If you are sincerely interested in protecting your family's future, when do you think is a good time to start?

After you die, do you want your money to go toward building missiles, building hospitals or to your kids? If you do nothing, a large portion will go towards building missiles.

What does your income pay for now? Who is dependent on your paycheck? Who would pay the bills if you were not around?

What services for your family do you or your spouse perform? Which services would have to be replaced?

Who would take care of the children wile your spouse was at work?

What long range family goals would have to be modified if something were to happen to you? (Education for you children, spouse's retirement etc.)

When you need more life insurance in the future, What if you can't get it because your health has changed?

Are you planning to provide for your wife for as long as you live or as long as she lives?

How much is your family's future worth to you? A thousand dollars? A million?

How much life insurance do you have now? How soon will you need more?

Is protecting your family's future and living comfortably after you retire of any interest to you at all?

If I offered you $100 to walk to New York, would you?

If there were $1,000,000 waiting for you when you arrived, you'd start walking right now wouldn't you?

If I could show you how to arrive at the $1,000,000 city by saving $100 per month, you would want to take that first step today, wouldn't you?

If you were ever going to start saving money, when do you think would be the best time to start?

Mr. Biz Owner, if you had died last night, how would your family get any money out of your business?

Mr. Biz Owner, how would you like to have someone waiting with money ready to buy your business from your family when you die?

Closing Questions

Can you see where this would help your family to save money?

Let me ask you a few questions about your health then we can see if you qualify.

Here's what we've found you need. Let me ask you a few questions about your health then we can see if you qualify.

Can you think of any other solution that would work better for you and your family than life insurance?

If you were to go ahead with this policy, would you prefer payment by check or pre-authorized checking?

When would be a convenient time for your medical exam?

What haven't I covered to your satisfaction?

Do you think that doing this would be the best thing for you family?

Is the immediate cost the most important factor in you decision or are you more concerned with the long term value?

Can you think of any reason - aside from the price - that you shouldn't have this right now?

Mr. _____, on a scale of 1 to 10, with 10 meaning you are ready to go ahead with this, where would you stand right now?

If you are at _____ right now, what would it take to move you to a 10?

If I could show you how this plan would pay for itself, would you want to get started right away?

Why don't we get this started?

How do you feel about this?

Does that make sense?

What do you think; do you want to go ahead with this?

Would you check this list and see if it covers your immediate needs?

This is an ideal savings plan, don't you think?

Which of these options is more/most important to you right now?

Is that the only thing holding you back?

How does that sound to you?

Why is that important to you?

Do you agree that this would save you money?

How do you feel about this?

Are you in agreement that this is at least a partial solution to your problem?

There might be some short term financial consequences but what do you think the consequences could be of not doing this?

Isn't this a great plan?

Do you want to handle this annually and take advantage of the savings or would paying monthly be more convenient for you?

This policy can give your widowed family a half decent chance at enjoying life and create a lot of wealth. And it's quite affordable. Why don't we go ahead with it?

Answers To Objections

I Can't Afford It

Suppose money was not a consideration, then would you buy?

The premium is not your problem; it's the solution to your problem. If you can't pay today, while you are still working, and it costs pennies on the dollar, how can you expect your wife to pay dollar for dollar when you're dead and gone?

I appreciate your honesty in telling me you can't afford it. But let me ask you this, you do like what this can do for your family don't you? Then if you could afford it, would you buy it today? I'm not asking you to spend any more money than you are already spending. What I am asking is for you to change your spending habits a little and start paying yourself first to protect your family's future. Instead of seeing your money go for that extra trip to McDonald's or that extra six pack each week, you'll have something to show for your money.

Our budgets prevent us from doing many things. Most people try to prioritize how they spend their money. If you feel this coverage is important, I am confident we can find a way in which you can remodel your home in addition to purchasing this needed protection.

I think I understand what you mean. You're saying that your living expenses are so high that there is nothing left over for life insurance premiums. Is that about right? If it takes all of your income for your family to live now, what are they going to do with little or no income after you're gone?

We're talking about necessities not luxuries. Let's review your budget and I'll bet we can find a lot of things that are less important than a college education for your children or your family's ability to continue living in the way they're accustomed in the event of your premature death.

If your father were to say to you, "Son, I'm flat broke. Can you give me $3.00 a day to live on? What would you tell him? Would you give it to him? Of course you would. Can't you see that's what we're talking about here? If you would do that for your father, why wouldn't you do that for your widow and kids?

If the doctor said that you, or a member of your family, would have to go to the hospital for an operation, would you say you couldn't afford it, or would you find a way to pay for it? The answer is obvious. Right now, the plan I'm recommending is as essential to your family and yourself as an operation.

When we say we 'can't afford' something, aren't we usually speaking of luxuries? But life insurance is no luxury. It represents food, clothing, shelter, education and basic income for you family if something should happen to you.

Can your family afford to be without this protection? Can your family afford to be without income if something should happen to you? This plan represents only a few dollars a week outlay. In terms of the things your family would have to do without. Wouldn't you agree this is a small sacrifice to make?

All of us can afford something if we want it badly enough. It's obvious that I haven't done a good job of making you want this plan that much. But it seems to me that the premium payments we're talking about here are insignificant compared to the price your dependents would have to pay without this plan.

People almost never buy all the life insurance they need at once. They add more, piece by piece as their incomes permit. Unless of course they don't live long enough to buy the next policy. In that case, they have bought all the live insurance they'll ever own. I'm merely suggesting you take the next step toward what will eventually be a complete life insurance program.

Except for money, can you think of any reason not to go ahead right now?

You think the price is too high? Could you be more specific?

I Don't Want To Take On Any More Obligations

I can understand that, but have you looked at it this way? I'm not suggesting you add any obligations. I'm offering you a chance to discharge some of those you already have - those you willingly took on when you married and started raising a family. By owning this life insurance program you will actually have fewer obligations, not more.

If you don't buy this life insurance, you'll still have all the obligations you have now, Isn't that right? Well have you thought of it this way? If you do buy this program you'll have fewer obligations. You'll be transferring some of your most serious ones form your own shoulders to the broad shoulders of my company. I mean the obligations of a permanent home for your family – and income to live on - and education for your children - and money for new clothes, new bikes and braces. Not to mention your obligation to the older person you will be one day - if you live. I'm not asking you to take on any more obligations. I'm here to remove some of those you already have.

Yes, I'm sure that like most people, you have the normal number of current debts, unpaid bills and the like. But wouldn't they still have to be paid if you die? And isn't your wife the one who would have to pay them? Well then, don't you want to make sure that after paying off your obligations, your spouse will have an income that's enough to live on?

The reason you need this coverage is so your family can meet those obligations, even if something should happen to you. You would want them to be able to do that, wouldn't you?

I Don't Need It

You may not need more insurance ... but your family will need more money when you die.

People often say they don't need insurance. They have to realize though that not buying coverage doesn't make the risk go away --- it just makes them the world's smallest insurance company

You're right, you don't need it right now, you're not dead yet. I can guarantee you this however, life insurance is like a parachute; if you ever need it and don't have it, and you'll never need it again. Tell me, do you carry a spare tire in your car?

If you had said you were glad I called because you needed to buy insurance today, I'd be very surprised. If you don't need to buy today, I'll wait until you are ready. Meanwhile, I'd like to meet you and tell you about the services I provide.

I Want To Think About It

Obviously you would not take the time to think this over unless you were really interested. Let's make a quick list. What points do you need to consider?

I encourage you to think it over. However, I recommend that you be covered while you are thinking about it. It will take four to six weeks to issue the policy. Let's complete the application and bind the coverage today. This way your family will be protected, while you're thinking about the coverage

Let me ask you a question. If you could have it for nothing would you take it? Well, I guess what you really want to think about is how much you can set aside for this plan, isn't that true? If I asked you to set aside $1.00 per month, you would say that was no problem, true? However if I asked you to set aside $100 a month, you would probably say it was a problem, true? Well there must be somewhere between $1.00 and $100 you can set aside.

At the moment you have only $25,000 of whole life, which is just about enough to bury you. If you were to be killed tomorrow, your children would never get to college; and over the years they might become quite accustomed to standing in the unemployment lines. Your wife will probably have to go on welfare for 3 to 5 years until she learns enough office skills whereby she can support the baby sitter and the two kids.

That's good; but let's thinks it over together. Let me clear up some important points. For $___ a month, paid by you, my company will guarantee to pay your family a total of $_____, even if you die tonight. On the other hand, if you live to age 65, we'll return an amount equal to substantially more than all the premiums you have paid. And if you should become disabled somewhere along the way, my company will keep your insurance in force and pay your premiums for you. That's a wonderful plan. Don't you agree?

That's all right. But while you're thinking it over, there's someone else who has to do some thinking too... my company's underwriting department. It won't do you much good to give this a lot of thought only to discover that the company has come up with some negative thoughts. Let's make sure you have something concrete to think about by arranging a medical exam for you this afternoon. Let me call the doctor to see what time is available.

In running my business, I have often found myself on the opposite side of the table from a salesman and have made that very same statement. Over a period of time, I came to realize that whenever I asked for time to 'think it over' I was really saying one of three things. In the first place, I might really want to think it over because I had some questions that had not been answered, if this is what you are saying, I'd be glad to answer those for you right now. Or I might really be saying, I'm not interested in any way, but I just didn't want to hurt the salesperson's feelings, though I had no intention of considering the proposal any further. I can respect your decision and would only ask that if this is the case, please tell me how and save us both time. Or I might ask time to think it over when I really had another objection. Again, I would only ask that you be honest with me, as I have been with you, and allow me the opportunity to answer whatever questions or objections you may have.

Isn't it true that, in the business world, the ability to make decisions is important to advancement? It's just as true in personal life.

Here's a plan that you agree is a good one. Everything you told me indicates that you can handle the premiums without difficulty. I'm here, you're here, Why don't we go ahead and get this plan started right now?

Let's think it over together. Perhaps there's something that I didn't fully explain. It's really easier for you to decide while I'm here to answer questions, and while all the facts are fresh in your mind. Let me suggest this, it takes several weeks to find out whether or not the company can offer you this plan. Let's find out if you can qualify. While you're thinking about it, give me a check for the first month's premium and the worst that can happen is that you will receive two months of protection for one month's premium. Let's go ahead, okay?

Stand up and say: Fine, I'm going to run and get a cup of coffee; I'll be back in 5 minutes, so you folks go ahead and talk it over. When you come back say: "Which way did you decide would be best for us to provide this plan for you - Monthly, automatic check or annual payments?"

I'd like To Wait

Waiting doesn't solve your problem; it only postpones it. You have a right to postpone it. But if you postpone solving your problem too long do you know who will have to solve it? Your spouse.

All right, if you'd like to wait awhile that's certainly your decision to make. But would you mind telling me what you're waiting for? Are you waiting for good health? I don't think you'll have any trouble qualifying physically. Are you waiting until you have a need? We've already agreed the need won't be any less later on than it is now. Are you waiting for more money? You appear to be a person who could put this program in force, if you only would. Are you waiting until you are a year older? In that case the premium rate will go up and the whole plan will cost more than it does today. Tell me honestly, what are you waiting for?

You say you'd like to wait a few months. If you don't need additional life insurance now, the chances are you won't need it then, and I don't want to sell you anything you don't need. On the other hand if you need it then, you probably need it now - and every day you wait you're gambling with your family's future. These are pretty high stakes aren't they?

I'll be happy to talk to you about this later. But let's think about it. If it's really a good idea to have then, isn't it even better now? Every man becomes uninsurable sooner or later. You could be uninsurable now and, if so, we've already waited too long. Let's get started now and find out if we can get it for you.

Why is next month a better time? What will be more advantageous then? What's going to happen between now and then that will make a difference?

OK, if I call back next month and you're not there (dead), who should I ask for?

Among others, there are two good reasons to act now:
a. Your rate is going up.
b. Something may happen to make you uninsurable.

Do you feel this is the right plan for you and your family? Have you ever regretted making a decision that you felt to be the right one?

I Can Do Better With My Money

Tell me what happened in the stock market in the last couple of years. It was up, fine. Then it was down, not so fine. That's not the kind of foundation I want for myself and my family, or for the people depending on me. I'd like to be sure that when I'm gone there's something there --- a real foundation --- something my people can depend on.

You can buy other types of property whether you're seven or seventy. You can buy them whether you're in good health or bad. You can buy them at any time if you have money. But the only time you can buy life insurance is when you're insurable. If you wait too long, it may be too late to buy the only property that can take care of your family's basic need immediately, and automatically accumulate dollars for your own basic need in the future

Perhaps you can, if you live. But nobody can guarantee that can they? Your economic value to your family is tremendous. If you live you'll earn thousands of dollars, most of which will be spent on their well being. But if you die, something will have to replace your earning power. That something is life insurance. No other kind of property can create an immediate estate and guarantee to take care of your family if you're not here to do it yourself.

I'm sure you can, there's just no question about it. I have some good speculative investments myself. But, economists tell us that each investor should have a balance between guaranteed and speculative investments. Money invested in this plan is guaranteed to be there whether we live, die, or become disabled. It's the only investment in the world that will continue after you become disabled. Many men have gotten rich by transferring guaranteed dollars into speculative investments when the right opportunity comes along. Starting this guaranteed plan of accumulating capital can be the springboard to your financial success, providing the money to invest in speculative investments when those once in a lifetime opportunities come along.

This is the very reason you should buy permanent life. Many people believe this, but historically the major ways to accumulate wealth have been: inherit it, marry it, buy real estate, or permanent life.

What will you invest in? Will it be tax deferred? Will it be guaranteed?

Locking you into a reasonable rate and 100% security overcomes your procrastination and lack of investing skill; permanent life guarantees wealth.

My Wife Can Get Remarried or Go Back To Work

If I died tomorrow, I would hope very much that my wife would find a person she could love and that she could remarry. I honestly believe that the lord meant for us to love as man and wife, rather than alone. I would certainly hate to think that she had to get remarried though.

Do you want to make that compulsory? Remember, with three kids she isn't going to be quite the catch she was when you married her. Why don't you give her a choice?

Why force your wife back into the marriage market, for lack of economic independence, when her soul is burdened with rich memories of you?

You are fortunate to have such a good wife. But is it best for your young children if she leaves home everyday to go to work? Are you sure she'll have the money to pay for the same care and attention she gives to your children. And will money really replace her daily love and care?

Psychologists tell us that it's a tragedy for a child to lose a parent. But they go further to say that it is a catastrophe for a child to lose both parents, and if one parent dies and the other works, as far as the child is concerned, he has lost both parents. Wouldn't it make sense, as a matter of fact, for her to work now, if necessary to help pay for additional capital needed, rather than attempt to work after your death?

It's wonderful that your wife's family is wealthy. I happen to be in that unique position myself. But I'm sure that, like me, you wouldn't want your friends to say that you wife had to go home and live with them, whether she wanted to or not.

I Have Enough Life Insurance

You don't plan on being dead long!

Economists tell us that most families can stay within their own world if they can be provided about 60% of the income that they had before the husband died. Staying in their own world means allowing the children to stay in their own schools, retain their friends and neighborhood when familiar surroundings are needed most. Our rough calculations indicate that your present assets simply will not do this.

When you die, you're going to be dead a long time. $100,000 spread out over a long time for your family, isn't very much money, is it?

Is that all you'd want your wife and kids to have when you're gone?

That's wonderful. Many people aren't that fortunate. May I ask you a question? If you were in your spouse's place and your husband (wife) died, could you maintain your home, educate your children and live as comfortably as you would like on the income from your present insurance?

I Have Life Insurance at Work

The life insurance you have at work is part of your total financial plan. But don't put all your eggs in one basket. You could be laid off. You could decide you no longer want to work for that company. You're healthy today, but what if you leave your present job, try to buy life insurance and find you're unhealthy and uninsurable?

What will happen to your group insurance if you change jobs? If you are laid off? If you go into business for yourself? When you retire? If it's like most group plans, you'll have no insurance. One advantage to owning your own policy in addition to your group coverage is that you have control. This plan will also help you accumulate value and build for the future, something your group coverage can't do

 Are you allowing your employer to dictate the amount of coverage you should have or shouldn't have?

Generally your coverage is going to be based on your salary or position. But there might be one person who has 5 children and a spouse and another person who is single at the same salary and given the same amount of insurance. The amount of insurance you have at work has nothing to do with the amount of insurance you probably need.

I Have a Friend or Relative in the Business

Great. How much life insurance have you purchased from him?

Many people have told me that they don't want their relatives to know about their personal business. Life insurance is a personal product. Some relatives are too close to analyze it objectively. On the other hand, I can be objective and everything you say will be kept confidential.

That's fine, however, it will cost you nothing to find out what I have to offer that might be valuable to you.

That's great, but you know, most people don't want to handle their business on a friendship business. They prefer to keep their financial affairs on a strictly business basis and not have friends involved in their personal business.

I've learned from sad experience that many of my friends were using me as an excuse to put off other life insurance agents, even before I talked with them about life insurance. I was reluctant to see them about it because we are friends. I suspect your agent friend may have the same reluctance. But I'm here and would appreciate the chance to tell you my story.

Most people have a relative or very close friend in the life insurance business. Many of them have told me that they would rather not have relatives knowing about their personal affairs. For example, most of our policyholders take advantage of the loan values in their policy for different purposes, and many of them would just as soon not have their relatives involved in their personal matters. It's sort of like a doctor. My wife would not like to go to one of our close friends who happen to be a doctor, simply because she knows him well.

Does that mean that regardless of how interesting a plan I was to show you, you would buy only from your friend? Are you obligated to buy all the rest of your life insurance from your friend?

I've never met a person who didn't have a friend in the life insurance business. But I've also never met a person who objected to having two friends in the business. Besides, what I'm here to discuss is not necessarily concerned with your buying life insurance

now. I've come to meet you and offer my
services. I have some financial information I
think you'll find interesting.

I'm not surprised. Most people have a life
insurance agent from whom they've purchase
before. What I would like to do is make a
direct comparison with our company and the
policies which you own now to see how good
his recommendations have been to date.

I'm Insurance Poor

Then you must already own a substantial amount of insurance. What company issued your present policy?

You're really insurance rich. You just don't realize how fortunate you are to have good health and the income to support a good life insurance program. And even more, you they don't realize what good property you own- or how much of your premium dollars go to build cash values. You'd be interested to talk about the life insurance you own now, wouldn't you?

I used to feel the same way until I compared what my life insurance would do for my family if I died, with what my earning ability will do for them while I'm living. Let me compare your present life insurance against your family's needs. Then you can know just how insurance poor you are.

Did you ever hear people say they are 'stocks and bonds poor' or 'mutual funds poor' or 'savings account poor'? Of course not. Life insurance is simply another method of accumulating cash, but one which also includes a unique protection feature.

I want to talk it over with...

I've found that when it comes to life insurance, there are three kinds of spouses. The first is the one who really doesn't want to talk about the possibility of his or her mate's death. The second is the spouse who sees life insurance as a competitor for a new car or vacation trip. And the third is the one who says it's up to you. But I've found that all of these spouses have at least one thing in common. Down deep inside they say to themselves, I'm glad my spouse loves me enough to do this for me.

That's a good idea, I think you should. But wouldn't it be a good idea if we all talked it over together? After all, he or she is certain to have some questions I could answer on the spot. And in anything as important as buying life insurance, I believe everyone should have a clear understanding of the problem and the solution.

Great, but in the meantime let's go ahead and get things started. When I deliver the policy, let's include your wife so she can understand exactly what you've done

That may be a good idea, but let me give a word of caution. I had a friend who had the same impulse - and he did go home and tell his wife what he planned to do. She was delighted with the additional security the suggested insurance would give her. Then the medical exam came back. He got insurance all right, but with a heavy rating, and his wife is still losing sleep worrying about his condition. Wouldn't it be best to spare your wife possible anxiety by finding out if you can get insurance before you talk with her about it?

Your lawyer keep keeps you on the right track and protects you from lawsuits, and your accountant figures out how much you owe, but when the chips are down ... they don't pay the bills they just figure them out. I pay the bills.

My wife doesn't need life insurance

You feel your wife's life should not be insured? Let me ask you a question... How much money would it cost you per month to pay someone to do the work she does? For example: childcare, shopping, laundry, cooking, etc.

I think you can agree that it would be a huge financial burden to purchase the services that your wife provides. I think life insurance on your wife is essential. Don't you?

I'm young, I don't need life insurance.

It's best to start a life insurance program while you're young and healthy. You can add to it as your needs change.

If I told you that you were going to die tomorrow; would you still say that you were too young?

Just like you didn't think you needed an education while you were in school, you secured it for your future anyway. You will want to have life insurance in the future , I guarantee it.

I'm worried about inflation

Do you carry more fire insurance on your home than was carried ten years ago? Well it's the same with life insurance. It's absolutely necessary that larger amounts of life insurance be carried because of inflation.

It seems to me that your principal concern should not be inflation but deflation. Think of all the problems your family would face trying to live on the amount of income they'd have if you weren't here. For them, that would be real deflation.
Life insurance like this is the only property outside of cash savings and government bonds) in which the dollar value is certain. Everything else you own can fluctuate in value. That is certainly true of your house, which is probably you largest single investment. You have no idea now of what it will bring if you put it on the market a given number of years from now.

Don't you agree that a widow or widower is not nearly as concerned about receiving inflated or deflated dollars as about receiving enough dollars? Everything must be purchased with money. Isn't it how many dollars can be counted on, rather than how

much these dollars are worth that is of
primary importance?

Speaking of inflation, do you realize that the
greatest opportunity to capitalize on it is in
life insurance? If a person, aged 35, owns an
ordinary life policy and dies in the first year,
the premium dollar is inflated about 5000%!
If that person dies in the fifth year, the
premium dollar is inflated 1000%, in the tenth
year 500% and in the twentieth year there
would be an inflation of 250%. That's what I
call real inflation - the kind all breadwinners
would like to provide for their families

I'm not interested

I'm not surprised to hear you say that. I assume you mean you're not interested in buying more life insurance. But like most people you are interested in accumulating a cash fund aren't you?

That's all right; I can't expect you to be when you know nothing about me or the service I offer. I'm calling on you today to get acquainted, and let you know that I've helped your friend ___ solve a particular problem. When may I have just a few minutes to show you the kind of work that I'm doing? How about now, or will tomorrow be more convenient?

OK, but I have to give you the opportunity to say no. It is my responsibility as your insurance professional to at least tell you about the products available and offer some advice. If you don't have the opportunity to say yes or no, then I'm not doing my job.

I can understand that, I haven't shown you anything to interest you. But if you'll give me just ten minutes, I have an idea I think you'll like. If I don't arouse your interest in that time, I'll be on my way, fair enough?

You're probably not interested in life insurance as such. But I'm sure you're interested in...... giving your children a good education?...making sure that your family can stay in their home and continue their present standard of living even if something should happen to you?...providing an income for yourself in your retirement years?

I don't have any reason to think that you are. However, you may want or need to purchase more insurance sometime in the future. If so, I'd like to show you what I do so that when you are ready to buy, perhaps I can be of service to you.

Power Phrases

Power Phrases

The best kind of life insurance is the kind that is in force when you die.

The time to start thinking about retirement is now.

The chance you will die is one out of one.

Isn't it a great feeling to know that whether you live or die, your kid's college education is provided for?

If there is anything worse than a home without a mother, it's a mother without a home.

If you don't arrange to pay your estate taxes, your survivors may spend their entire lives buying your business back from the government.

It's far easier to pay for a college education over 10 or 15 years than it is in 4.

Life insurance enables a person to accomplish - immediately what otherwise would be the work of a lifetime.

The problem is not dying too young, but outliving your money.

Upon your death your estate will either have to sell or liquidate at a possible great financial loss, or else borrow the money to pay the taxes, if you make no plans.

Our birth certificates don't carry an expiration date. Now let's go ahead with this plan.

I help people plan for a sound financial future while protecting themselves and their loved ones for the present, through insurance.

There are basically four financial catastrophes that could occur. Early death, disability, economic depression, and not saving enough money. Life insurance is the only hedge against all four catastrophes, not just the first.

You need to plan for the worst and hope for the best.

One of two things is certain; either you will live or die. If you live, you will need money. If you die your family will.

You can't take it with you. Did you ever see a hearse with a U-Haul?

Why leave everything to chance when you could leave something to your family.

The winners at poker and life insurance are the ones who are in the game at the end.

If you won $100,000 jackpot at the casino, would you stop working and live on the $100,000 the rest of your life? That's exactly what you're asking you're family to do.

Do you mind if I insure your $500,000 home for $100,000? Then why only insure one fifth of yourself?

If every wife knew what every widow knows, every husband would own more life insurance.

Life insurance is the last thing on earth a man wants - and then he can't get it.

Making money is easy; keeping it is the hard part.

It's not a man's chance of dying that is so great, but the consequences of his death that are so significant.

Someone always pays for life insurance. It is bought with sacrifices. Either you sacrifice a little today or your family sacrifices a lot tomorrow.

This $100,000 policy will protect your family ... for only $100 per month ... and will eventually help send your two kids to college.

A man buys life insurance not because he might die, but because someone else must go on living.

When you die the accountant and lawyer will apologize and sent their bills. I bring money.

There are only two questions about money; will it be there and how much?

A permanent life insurance policy is the greatest love letter ever written.
Now you can say to your banker; will you lend me the money or should I get it from my life insurance policy?

I know you want your wife and kids to be able to live in the same home, have the same friends, and be able to go to the same church and schools, whether you live or die.

It is better to have life insurance and not need it, than to need it and not have it.

Nobody likes being old or broke, but being both is terrible.

Most investments are a crap shoot. That doesn't mean you can't do well, or that you shouldn't invest. It means you should invest with dollars you can afford to lose, or at least do without for a little while.

Don't take life too seriously; none of us are going to get out of it alive.

Do you know what the difference between an old man and an elderly gentleman is? Income.

Most people are convinced that if they have enough productive time, they will make enough money to take care of their families. No one however is guaranteed the time. That's what makes insurance so perfect. If you don't get the time, we give you the money. If you get the time, we give you your money back!

You wouldn't buy term insurance if you knew you were going to live to be 85. It's actuarially computed not to be in force when you die!
Prospecting is like shaving; don't do it and one day you'll end up looking like a bum.

Your family will appreciate you for having provided them with this basic protection to take care of their living expenses and education in the event of your early demise. Your business friends will also appreciate the great investment side of this new policy; they may even be interested.
Success in life requires ability, opportunity and time. You have ability; you can make opportunity, only life insurance can guarantee it.

If I find a problem that is going to cost your family money, you need insurance. I will show you the price of doing something about it, and the price of doing nothing about it. I will show you that by doing nothing it will cost you dollars, but by doing something it will cost you pennies.

Let's look at your goals as an oak tree. There are two ways to climb an oak tree. You can climb limb by limb, or you can just sit on an acorn. Which one do you think is the most practical?

People don't want to buy life insurance; they want to buy what life insurance does.
If there is one thing a person can't argue with in an insurance policy, it is the fact that if he dies in the first year, he will have acquired more money than he possibly could in any other investment.

I sell contracts for time and money. I can't guarantee the time but I can guarantee the money.

One hundred percent of your family's problems can be solved for just three percent of your income. Who can do better?

We all must die someday, never at the right time. Always at the wrong time. I can give you money to complete your plans.

You look good on the outside ... how about the inside? Let's take a look, and if you are as good as you seem to be, I'll be back.

Thoughtful people plan for three generations. Thoughtless people plan for Saturday night.

Life insurance buys you time - How? by creating money. Money that can guarantee that your spouse can raise your family, continue a business, pay off your home, educate your children, secure a spouse's welfare, complete all of your dreams for your family - even if you're not here.

Were you aware a divorced woman's standard of living will drop to one half of what it was within one year after her divorce? The same statistic applies to a young widow.

What life insurance does best is deliver money at a time when your family needs it most.

Term insurance is designed to die before you do.

This is an estate tax table. It'll show you how much of what you own isn't yours.

I have never met anyone who has too much money in their retirement fund.

Put yourself in my position. If you were handing my widow a check for the amount of life insurance you have now, and she asked if she will be alright, what you would say.

Insurance is the closest thing to getting something for nothing I've ever found.

Once you're dead, you're dead.

When you buy a pair of pants or a pair of shoes, you just can't buy any pair, you make sure they fit. Like a custom tailor, I make life insurance fit.

No one ever died with too much money.

Why insure everything you own for what its worth except your life, your most important asset? Each man is a money making machine, and should be insured for what he's worth.

Life insurance is not a windfall. You're not going to make your family rich. It's bad enough losing a member of your family, but if they have to struggle financially it's a double whammy.

Let's use insurance to keep together what you put together.

Everybody is going to buy life insurance someday.

I want to help you get what you want.

Did you know that about 1 man in 12 who wants to buy life insurance can no longer buy it because of their health?

Put me on your payroll. The day you walk out, Ill walk in and pay your bills.

Do you know anyone who has a lease on life? It isn't a question of if; it's a question of when.

We come into this world totally dependent, financially and physically. All too often we leave the same way.

When you die your family will go on living ... but with what ... because the bulk of your income comes from your earnings and not from your assets. When you stop, your earnings stop.

To successfully accumulate wealth, you must save first and spend what's left over, not the other way around.

To save a lot of money, you have to save a lot of money.

This may be the last time you get to buy life insurance. Let's make sure it's adequate.

Happily ever after doesn't just happen.

Your wife is not going to care about what kind of insurance you had. She'll care about how much insurance you had.

Term insurance is like wetting the bed, it gives you temporary relief but sooner or later you've got to get up and do something about it.

Let me show you how life insurance works. Do you have a dollar? Let me have it for a second. (Hand prospect a $100 bill) Do you have another? (Give prospect another) Then say: the more of these you give me the more of those I'll give your family if something were to happen to you.

There's a unique process I'd like tell you about. Let's say you give me a check for a month's premium. While you're thinking about us, we're thinking about you. I will call to tell you if your application has been approved or not, and you can tell me if you've decided in that month's time, or any time before that, that you don't want the insurance, I'll refund your money. On the other hand, if you do want the insurance, we've already got the policy in force and have saved a considerable amount of time. What's unique about this is that it's a 'no loss' situation for you. The minute you give me a check, you're insured. You can see that it's possible that you might decide that you didn't want the insurance, but before you were able to reach me, and unforeseen accident took your life. We would still pay the death benefit. I think this is certainly putting the ball in your court.

(Open your briefcase with a thousand dollar bill in it) Point to it and say - That's what I sell. This thousand dollar bill comes in packages of a hundred. How many do you want?

(Pick up the telephone and bang the receiver down three times and say): Did you hear that? Do you know what that sound was? That was opportunity knocking and you shouldn't miss out on it!

If I told you that there was a building under construction and you could invest in it for

$50,000, and that when the building was finished you $50,000 investment would be guaranteed to be worth $500,000, wouldn't you want to make that investment? If I further told you that the $500,000 could come to your family tax free, wouldn't you want to know where this building is and how to invest in it? Well metaphorically speaking, such a building does exist and I'm going to show you where it is and how you can share in this fantastic investment opportunity.

There exists no other method that legally permits and guarantees the results you will certainly realize from this investment.

Suppose I told you I was with the Internal Revenue Service and for today only we are offering a special on estate tax rates that will effectively reduce your taxes by 90%. Furthermore, if you will give me 3 million today, I will give you a receipt that shows you to have paid the entire tax on you $50 million estate. At any other time these taxes will equal 27.5 million, but for today you can pay them for only 10% of that amount. Wouldn't you rush to take advantage of this incredible offer? You would have to wait in line. The IRS does not make this offer. But in effect,

the same end result can be accomplished by
my insurance company

With your current estate of $10 million, you
can expect to pay 50% in estate taxes. But
with a guaranteed 10 to 1 return on an
investment in a life insurance policy, based
on current assumptions, you can pay the total
$5 million tax assessment using only
$500,000. At age 60, that $500,000 will
purchase a policy worth $5 million. In effect
the life insurance policy pays the taxes on
your estate for a cost to you of 10 cents on the
dollar

To Order Additional Copies
of this book please visit:

www.lifesalesammo.com